Amelia Island
and
Fernandina Beach

by

Roger Moore

Photographs Naturally, Inc.

and

Ron Kurtz

The Amelia Island Museum of History

2008

Acknowledgements

Thank you to the following who contributed
to the publication of this book:

Janet Anderson, Paul Massing, Edith Doerr Moore, Donald Shaw, Jan Johannes,
Larry Bechan, Karen Taylor, Calvin Atwood, Carol Ann Atwood, Mary L. Kurtz, Robert Fisher,
Christina Nelson, Heather Dornbrock, Marlene Schang, Bonnie Sovereign, Lori Sage, Lynette
Blackwelder, Myers R. Kurtz, Ronald F. Shenk, Deon Lawrance Jaccard and the
Board of Trustees of the Amelia Island Museum of History, past, present and future…

Design: Chris Hamilton
Copyright Pending, All Rights Reserved
Printed in China
Sixth Edition
ISBN # 0-9710343-0-3
Published By Photographs Naturally, Inc.
Amelia Island, Florida

The typeface used throughout this book is Garamond (Regular, Italic, and Bold),
created by Claude Garamond of France in 1532 during the French Renaissance.

A portion of the proceeds from each book contribute to the support of the
Amelia Island Museum of History, Fernandina Beach, Florida

Cover: Amelia Island, where the land meets sand, and the sea meets infinity in the distant horizon.

Inside Cover: A Barred Owl (Strix varia) muses over his island kingdom where more than 175 species of birds can be identified.
It is a birder's paradise.

Table of Contents

RON KURTZ

Though born in Pittsburgh, Pennsylvania, Ron spent much of his early life as a self proclaimed "Army Brat." His father's postings took the family from Wurtzberg, Germany to Washington, D.C., and many places in between. He attended Hiram College in Hiram, Ohio, graduating from New York University.

His professional life began as a Fourth Grade teacher, later becoming Director of Continuity for a radio station. After serving as the General Manager of the Actors' Company of Pennsylvania, he began a career in residential and commercial interior design, with a focus on clients who were advanced collectors of 18th and 19th century decorative arts.

In 1994 he moved from Lancaster, Pennsylvania, to Amelia Island, where he served as a volunteer docent, a member of the Board of Trustees and as the Direcor of the Amelia Island Museum of History until 2001.

ROGER MOORE

A native of upstate New York, Roger served as a photographer with the Naval Group China during WW II. After earning a degree in Engineering from the University of Rochester, he began a career in construction contracting, eventually forming his own bridge building company, Nichols Long and Moore Construction Corporation, based in Buffalo, New York. In spite of his active professional life, he claims no direct relationship to his famous "007" namesake!

Roger and his wife Edie retired to Amelia Island in 1990, where he has since enthusiastically photographed the abundance of natural beauty to be found on the island. His work is exhibited with other artists at the Island Art Association, which is located in the heart of the Historic District of Fernandina Beach. He taught photography at Florida Community College, Nassau Institute for Community Education.

Photograph: Paul Massing

Ron Kurtz (Left) and Roger Moore (Right)

Roger Moore

Photographs Naturally, Inc.

and

Ron Kurtz

The Amelia Island Museum of History

History, Eight Flags

Chapter I

One fine morning, shortly after we began working on the book, Roger met a Brown Pelican (Pelecannus occidentalis) perched on the docks of the City Marina at the foot of Centre Street. Camera in hand, Roger captured fleeting images as the pelican posed and held for each click of the shutter.

A ballet of frozen moments emerged. The first shot in the sequence seemed to indicate a backward glance was in order. What better way to enjoy the visual pleasures ahead than to arm yourself with insights gleaned from the island's glorious past?

THE 8 FLAGS OF AMELIA ISLAND

France: 1562 to 1565,
and 1795

Spain: First Spanish Period:
1565 to 1763
Second Spanish Period:
1784 to1821, with interruptions!

England: 1763 to 1783

Patriots' Rebellion: 1812

Green Cross of Florida: 1817

Mexican Republic: 1817

United States of America:
Territorial Period: 1821 to 1845
Statehood as the 27th State: 1845 to present,
with one interruption

Confederate States of America:
1861 to 1862

THE 6 NAMES OF AMELIA ISLAND

Napoyca: Before 1562
Isle de Mai: 1562 to 1565
Santa Maria Island: 1565 to1736

Amelia Island: 1736 to the Present
(2 interruptions):

Egmont: 1763 to1783
The Republic of Amelia: 1817

To those of you who choose to hear, Amelia Island whispers her story with every passing breeze winding its way through twisted branches of water oaks and sea olives. Every crash of a wave upon her shore holds the promise of treasure pulled from the ocean's depths, whether shells and ancient sharks' teeth, or riches from the New World that failed to make the perilous journey back to the Old. No matter where your footsteps lead you on the island, others have walked before you...and others will follow, as your voice blends with those that tell a continuing tale of adventure on Amelia Island.

Echoes of times past are reflected in the sights that greet today's visitors. The photographs in this volume are true to the artist's vision, but they also offer untold riches to anyone who has chosen to listen to the story told by the wind and the waves.

As the Ice Age ended, the original settlers of our continent arrived, having crossed the Bering land bridge from northeastern Asia. Melting glaciers caused a gradual rise in the sea level, and the face of our planet changed. Twelve thousand years ago the ocean surged upon a distant shore. As far as the eye could see from what would later be known as Amelia Island, the peninsula stretched to the horizon in all directions. Florida's first inhabitants of the coastal region lived for thousands of years on ground that is now covered by the Atlantic Ocean. The water was relentless. As the sea receded, portions were trapped between what had been mainland dunes and the newly created shoreline. Thus, a system of barrier islands evolved as a buffer between the fragile North American coastline and the onslaught of the Atlantic Ocean. Underwater archaeologists and divers will be the ones to explore the story of Florida's first settlers.

Even before these events took place, our small portion of the planet was evolving. Deposits of ancient shells, sand and silt would be combined to create sedimentary limestone. This would serve as our island's foundation. The shimmering quartz beaches on the eastern shore are the result of erosion from the Allegheny Mountains, carried southward by streams and rivers, ultimately washed ashore by the vast ocean's currents.

From the sea oats that help to hold the dune system in place to woodlands of live oaks, palmettos, southern magnolias and red cedars, the land gives way to scrub-pinelands and mixed broad-leaved forests. The western shore is lined with a cordgrass tidal marsh following the brackish, salt-laden Amelia River that separates us from the mainland.

Amelia Island is a veritable Noah's Ark. 175 species of birds, many of them migratory, can be identified. 91 of the species breed here. From the Great Horned Owl and Pileated Woodpecker, to the Great Blue Heron and the Painted Bunting, observant birders have garnered a wealth of sightings. Exquisite butterflies abound in the wild and in the island's many cultivated gardens. In addition to alligators, you can see the nests of Loggerhead Turtles and Gopher Tortoises. Fishermen delight in our vast resources of everything from Blackfin Tuna and Flounder, to Sea Trout and Amberjack. A rare but unforgettable sight is the glimpse of a Right Whale in our coastal waters. These giant mammals were first sighted here and recorded by French explorers in the sixteenth century.

While aspects of our ecology can be discovered on other barrier islands, one thing sets us apart from all of the others. The forces of nature that formed the island gave it the deepest natural harbor on the southeastern coast. Our spacious harbor could, and sometimes did, accommodate 400 ships at anchor. A fully laden Galleon sat suspended 15 feet below the water's surface, while our harbor measured about 17 feet deep at low tide. Proximity to the fresh-water of the St. Marys River was also crucial to our commercial development. For centuries one of the scourges of the sea was the Toredo Bivalve, often mistakenly referred to as a shipworm. The thick planks and supporting structure of their host ships proved to be a banquet for the Toredo Mollusk. It wasn't until the mid eighteenth century that the British began sheathing hulls in copper in an attempt to prevent this kind of damage. The only other thing that controlled them was fresh water. Wood hulled ships plotted their courses from the open ocean through the Cumberland Sound to the St. Marys River. The final leg of their journey was into Amelia Island's deep, protected waters. From 1562 our harbor mirrored the images of eight different flags, reflecting the best and worst of human intentions.

Another unique geographical aspect is our location on the "Georgia Bite." The continental coastline is indented, as if celestial teeth had taken a "bite" from the smooth southern shoreline between Georgia and Florida. In addition, the Gulf Stream heads directly toward the island before veering off to the northeast, guiding potentially damaging weather systems to the north. These two features have served us well in hurricane season.

We are able to trace the history of human habitation on Amelia Island back at least four thousand years. Hunter-gatherers first crossed the Amelia River to discover the island's bounty of wildlife and shellfish. The Timucuans, descendants of the St. Johns River valley people, created a society that flourished for thousands of years. (If you are wondering how to pronounce the tribal name, it goes as follows: (ti 'mü kü en), with the accent on the second syllable. Think of the "mooing" sound of a cow, and the "cooing" sound of a dove!) The tribal name, Timucuan, was not the one they used to describe themselves. Quite possibly, French explorers at the mouth of the St. Johns River heard references to "enemy" tribes further to the south, the Thimogona or Tymangoua. From the initial French usage to the Spanish who followed suit, the term was eventually employed by nineteenth century scholars to represent the language and the people who spoke it. Timucuans colonized an area ranging from the northern interior of Florida to southern Georgia, linked by a common language diversified by dialects. As with so many of civilization's earliest cultures, the language was spoken, not written. Piecing together their stories would be left to first hand observations of Europe's intrepid explorers. Interpretations by archaeologists and other scientists are continually enriching our understanding through research and new discoveries.

The Timucuans did not exist as isolated tribes; rather, they were a form of chiefdom, which evolved from a complex model of the Mississippian mound building culture. Political power was inherited through the female line of one "royal" family, the White Deer Clan. In this matrilineal society, a man married into his wife's family; therefore, it would be the eldest male child of the chief's sister who would be next in line to inherit the mantle of leadership. Lacking a male heir, the chief would be a woman. The European model was patrilineal, with the right to rule passing through the male line. Perhaps the concept of equal opportunity has its roots firmly planted in the heritage of our First Coast Native American ancestors!

Napoyca was the first recorded name of our island. By the mid sixteenth century there were 46 island villages ruled by a single chief, or cacique, who in turn was subject to the holata, or head chief, of Mocama, known today as Cumberland Island. These two areas were subject in turn to a greater authority: the holato ico of the St. Johns valley. Tribute, in the form of harvested crops and loyalty, was due each level of authority. The farming skills that supported their system of tribute were developed through interaction with the Apalachee tribes to the west. Twice during the long growing season, maize stalks supported the encircling tendrils of beans, while squash flourished between the stalks. Produce was stored in daub, or mud covered, structures located close to streams. Dugouts offered easy access. Food that was not given in trib-

ute or divided among the farmers as part of the harvest ritual was there for all in the village to share, according to need. This helped to create a structured society with ever increasing centralization of material wealth and power.

By traveling north down 14th Street and turning into that part of Fernandina Beach known as Old Town, you can visit a site of pre-historic Native American occupation. Nearly 40 acres are scattered with shell middens and shards, or sherds, which are broken pieces of pottery. Middens are the mounds that evolved as Native Americans disposed of refuse, including shells from nutritious mollusks. For centuries the remains of their single daily meal were tossed beside each dwelling. Family units consisting of one man, a woman and their children, lived together in circular, domed structures with thatched palmetto roofs. Homes with small garden plots spread outward from the much larger council house where the cacique and his several wives resided. A spacious ceremonial plaza was open to all. Archaeologists excavate these deep, many-layered mounds to develop a more detailed picture of ancient lifestyles.

The shards found on Amelia Island have another story to tell that is unique to our area. Pre-historic Indians living between the St. Johns River valley and the Savannah River were among the first groups to develop the technology and skill that enabled them to create and fire clay vessels. Prior to using the raw material it had to be tempered, or mixed with some other substance, to prevent cracking in the firing stage. Spanish moss was shredded, as was palmetto fiber. Later efforts included the use of sand. Around 500 B.C. a miraculous discovery was made at the mouth of the St. Johns River. A vein of clay was found that could be mined from its source and put to immediate use. Tiny molecules of prehistoric sponges from a time before man walked the land formed a tight bond that made it unnecessary to temper the clay with additional material. This "magic clay" has been found nowhere else in the continental United States.

Pots were made with shaped disks forming the base. Coils were built up to create the sides, which were then smoothed down. Hardwood paddles incised with a criss-cross pattern of squares were used to decorate the exterior and remove air pockets that might cause damage during firing in kindling-lined pits. The pattern evolved as a symbol of their belief system. Imagine a pyramid-like shape with the sun resting on the top. Lines came down from this central point and were attached to the four corners of a square base. The corners represented the quadrants: north, south, east and west. It was as if they were alluding to Napoyca, an island suspended in an infinite sea, yet tied by destiny to the path of the sun. Every time they carried water in one of their vessels, or cooked in one of the enormous clay pots that so intrigued the Europeans who had similar cauldrons of iron, they were reminded of their place in the universe. Even the mundane rituals of survival were elevated to a spiritual level.

Any discussion of artifacts, which are the objects of history that museums preserve and display to enlighten and delight their guests, presents a dilemma. With the many shards and remaining shell mounds still in existence on Amelia Island, the visitor and resident alike are faced with an ethical decision. As you explore the island, you are bound to find intriguing bits of history under foot. If you reach down to pick up some fascinating and curious remnant of the past, be aware that you are removing a priceless and irreplaceable piece of a puzzle. Part of the value of an artifact is in knowing exactly where it was found and how it relates to other pieces around it. At best it will become an artifact taken out of context, perhaps losing its significance in a drawer full of similar unidentified treasures in your home. At worst, the story that an archaeologist might have constructed had it been left in place can never be told.

The Timucuans celebrated the union of sea and land through yet another ritual. To make the ceremonial drink, cacina, they dried leaves of yaupon holly, which still grows wild on the island. The leaves were then steeped in heated water in a process much like we use to brew tea. The dark liquid, heavy with concentrated caffeine, was poured into a left-handed lightening whelk shell (Busycon contrarium.) It was a perfect drinking vessel, easy to grasp with a porcelain-like interior and a wide lip from which to drink. Depending on its size, the whelk shell could hold up to a quart of cacina. This potent potable brought about a heightened sense of reality in addition to an interesting side effect that inspired the Europeans to give yaupon holly its descriptive name: ilex (referring to the genus holly) vomitoria (referring to the "interesting" side effect triggered when consumption exceeded an individual's capacity!)

But what did these people look like? From observations in journals and reports sent back to Europe with accompanying period drawings, we can piece together an image that is supported by archaeologists' interpretations. Strong, healthy bodies were bronzed through heredity and constant exposure to the sun. Tattoos were a mark of stature within their society. Intricate patterns were made by piercing the skin with a sharp fragment of shell, infusing the wound with a natural coloring agent and covering it with bear grease to prevent infection. Ropes of natural pearls and shells were draped across their bodies. The long hair of the men was fashioned into a rounded, helmet-like shape and then dressed with more bear grease and accented with trophy tails and feathers gleaned from their hunting exploits. Men made breechcloths from animal skins. Women wove skirts from what we call Spanish moss, attaching separated filaments to hip-bands. Before being worn, the skirts were smoked to rid them of almost invisible red mites, followed by a treatment with sweet smelling herbs to neutralize the smell of smoke. Twenty-first century visitors who become fascinated by this member of the pineapple family and decide to take a sample home in their luggage, would do well to remember the wisdom and practices of the Timucuans!

For both men and women, the finishing touch was a pair of dried, dyed fish bladders strung on a sinew inserted through their pierced earlobes. One item of adornment that surprised the Europeans, perhaps giving rise to false expectations of the potential for material wealth, was the appearance of copper gorgets. The raw material of these neckpieces was a treasure gathered from trade routes extending deep into the continent, as far inland as the Great Lakes region. The "magic clay" from the mouth of the St. Johns River and shells gathered from our shore were some of the items that served as barter through which copper and many other precious items found their way back to Napoyca.

Timucuan traders were not the only explorers. The first journey of Columbus had irrevocably reversed the hourglass of history. With each European ship, the sands of time ran faster for the indigenous tribes. Two French vessels, known as carracks, brought with them the flag of their sovereign, Catherine de Medici, Queen Regent of France. Three golden fleur de lis suspended on a field of blue laid claim to Amelia Island on **May 3, 1562**. In deference to the time of year, Jean Ribault, captain of the expedition, named his discovery Isle de Mai, or Island of May. Napoyca's **FIRST FLAG**, that of **FRANCE**, heralded more than a new name. It marked the beginning of a progression of eight flags representing the dreams and ambitions of many men and nations. It also marked the beginning of the end of a civilization that had prospered for thousands of years. Among the bright, flashing bits of trade goods in the holds of their ships lurked a devastating cargo. Unknowingly, the Europeans brought diseases such as influenza and small pox, for which the Native Americans had no immunity. Tribal leaders were the first to approach the foreigners and the first to fall victim to disease. The sustaining structure of their society disintegrated as epidemics took their toll. One hundred years after the arrival of the French, the Timucua of Northeast Florida were all but extinct.

Those of you familiar with Florida's history may wonder why our island's first flag is not considered to be that of Spain. Unlike earlier journeys by other explorers, the Spanish crown sanctioned the exploits of Juan Ponce de Leon in 1513. La Florida was officially included in Spain's quest for vast territories and riches in the New World. It was named in honor of the calendar day of its claiming, Pascua Florida, during the Easter season. La Florida encompassed the entire continent of North America, yet by the mid-point of the century, no permanent Spanish colonies had been established. To claim and explore is entirely different than to claim and settle. Many ships had sunk, and Spanish lives had been lost to the perils of the sea. Spaniards also died at the hands of Native Americans who fought to protect their homeland from the invaders. Finally, in 1561, Phillip II of Spain issued a royal decree ending Spain's unprofitable venture in La Florida.

Civil war was raging in France during this era. The Catholics were struggling against a rising middle class of Huguenots, Protestant followers of John Calvin. Catherine de Medici was faced with challenges on all sides. She had grasped control of her country, serving as Queen Regent for her young son, Charles IX. News of Philip II's decree brought with it the perfect solution for the difficulties she faced. Since France had, for the most part, been excluded from the spoils of the New World, why not claim what Phillip II rejected? If the Protestant threat could be neutralized by removing some of them from France, why not man most of the expedition with Huguenots? It was a "win-win" proposition. If the ships sank, there would be that many fewer problematic Protestants! If the expedition were successful, France would share in the riches of the New World. Catherine sent two ships with mixed crews of Protestant and Catholic adventurers to claim La Florida. The issue of which flag to claim as our first was at a draw.

A combination of making landfall in 1562 and the founding of Ft. Caroline in 1564 won France the honor. It was here that French colonists gave birth to the first recorded generation of native-born European-Americans, pre-dating the birth of Virginia Dare, far to the north. One of the same issues that motivated the colonization efforts of the English Separatists in the early seventeenth century first inspired the French in the mid sixteenth century. Desire for religious freedom would help to expand the boundaries of the known world.

By driving down A1A South, which is also known as the Buccaneer Highway, you approach the Fishler/McArthur Bridge on the extreme southern tip of Amelia Island. Once on the bridge, you have crossed the border between Amelia Island and the city limits of Jacksonville. A half-hour drive takes you to a State Park commemorating the founding of Ft. Caroline.

Since a quest for knowledge and territory, in addition to encouraging French-Protestant immigration, were major objectives, Catherine de Medici included the cartographer Jacques le Moyne in the second expedition. He mapped the progress of the journey of exploration and the building of Ft. Caroline, as well as recorded the activities of the Native American inhabitants. His sketches, later translated into etching by the Flemish engraver-jeweler Theodore de Bry, are among the first we have of the New World as seen from a European perspective. Indicating abundant wildlife and fresh produce, including the ubiquitous grape, source of their ancestral libation, these pictures were obviously meant to entice adventurous Frenchmen to brave the Atlantic to be among the first citizens of France's growing empire in a land of opportunity.

Once the French acted by claiming La Florida and renaming it New France in 1562, the Spanish re-acted by launching a brutal advance in 1565. Pedro Menendez de Aviles off-loaded slaves from the holds of his ships and had them begin digging trenches that were to become the foundations of St. Augustine, the oldest surviving European-founded city in the continental United States. The French fleet, moored outside Ft. Caroline, sailed down the coast to rout the Spanish. The weather intervened, sinking the French ships. While the storm casualties were limited, Pedro Menendez sailed up to meet them at a spot that has been immortalized as Matanzas, which translates as "massacre." The word accurately describes what Menendez and his followers did to the shipwrecked French colonists.

Ft. Caroline was next to fall, with only a handful of French escaping and returning to Europe. Le Moyne was among the survivors. Nearly all of the French forces manning the fort were hung from live oaks outside the vanquished settlement. This proved to be a struggle not only between two nations for territorial rights, but also between the "Defenders of the True Faith" and the Protestant infidels. Spain re-named the captured fort San Mateo, and raised the **SECOND FLAG**, that of **SPAIN,** on **September 20, 1565**. By seizing control of Ft. Caroline and having just begun construction of St. Augustine, Spain could finally justify her previous claim. The First Spanish Period had begun, followed by 236 years of Spanish domination.

A challenge would follow almost immediately. In 1568 Dominique de Gourges set sail from France to avenge the brutality of the Spanish in La Florida. A former Spanish prisoner, de Gourges had both a personal and nationalistic motivation. Without the sanction of the crown, but supported by funds realized from donations and the sale of his property, he equipped three ships. Achieving landfall on the First Coast, de Gourges discovered a powerful ally. The Timucuans supported his cause due to the cruelty visited upon them by the Spaniards. The oaks outside Ft. Caroline would bear their second crop of "bitter fruit," as Spanish bodies hung by French hands replaced Huguenot bodies hung by Spanish hands less than three years earlier. De Gourges and his men set sail and left.

In an effort to further validate their claim, the Spanish established a mission on Amelia Island. It was called Santa Maria de Sena, and would serve as the inspiration for our second European name, Santa Maria Island. Many historians believe that the mission was located on the extreme north end of the island in the area of Old Town. Native Americans were considered a tool by the conquering European nations in their effort to control distant territories.

The Spanish Mission System had three major purposes. First, the Native Americans had to be converted to the Catholic Faith. Missions were also created to supply crops to support the survival of important population centers like St. Augustine. Central to the concept of legitimate territorial claims was the creation and maintenance of settlements. The most vital purpose was to serve as a "buffer zone" between Spain and any other nations that might offer a challenge to Spain's right to hold land in the New World. Later island missions included Santo Domingo, Santa Maria de Yamassee and the Doctrina of Santa Catalina de Guale. The last two were the focus of an archaeological dig started in 1986 within the grounds of the Amelia Island Plantation, a gated resort community on the south end of the island. The Yamassee and Guale that are referred to in the names of these two missions are tribes the Spanish brought to the island after the indigenous Timucuans had become extinct. The fact our small island would host so large a concentration of missions is a testament to the importance the island held in defining the territories of Spain.

Archaeology is a destructive science. Once identified, a potential site is divided into grids, and the slow task of digging begins, peeling back and studying each subsequent layer of earth before moving on to the next. The grids allow archaeologists to plot the exact location of artifacts. This information is enhanced by accurate measurements of the depth at which they were located. A list of the essential tools of wire-mesh screens, spoons and brushes should give you an idea of how slowly and carefully archaeologists proceed. Once the double

mission site had been thoroughly explored and interpreted, it was refilled and leveled to support the houses that would eventually be built. The human remains were re-interred with a Catholic ceremony at Bosque Bello Cemetery, adjacent to Old Town.

One of the artifacts unearthed by archaeologists from the Amelia Island Plantation excavation site was a bronze seal depicting Saint Catherine and her wheel of torture. Correspondence sent by the mission was secured by melted wax stamped with an impression carved into the flat surface of the seal. It is one of the few known artifacts of its kind to survive the passing of the Mission Era in the Western Hemisphere. The tale told by the seal and its significance to Amelia Island begins in the early morning hours of November 4, 1702.

Governor James Moore of South Carolina was convinced that shifting alliances in Europe would inspire former bitter rivals, France and Spain, to join forces to destroy England's hold on the Carolinas. This was more than 30 years before the as yet unfounded colony of Georgia would serve to protect the southernmost border of England's North American colonies. Governor Moore decided to take St. Augustine, burning all of the missions that lay in his path. The palmetto roofs and mud covered woven branch walls (wattle and daub) of the mission buildings proved to be the perfect fuel to support his scorched earth policy. In the chaos that ensued with his approach to Amelia Island early that fateful morning, the seal was dropped as the inhabitants escaped southward. Pursued by the English, they joined the Spanish and Christianized Native Americans who had deserted St. Augustine and fled to the safety of the fort guarding the city. In spite of a 53-day siege, Governor Moore failed to break their hold and had to return in defeat to South Carolina. This campaign of fire and death, followed by a second attempt two years later, brought a close to the Mission Period in La Florida many years before it ended in other Spanish territories.

As you can see, the early years of the eighteenth century brought many challenges to our island, but it was not until well after the mid-point of the century that Spain's flag would be replaced. The next challenge brought a delightful change we celebrate to this very day. It came at the hands of another Englishman. In 1733 James Oglethorpe founded the colony of Georgia, named for his sovereign, George II of England. Three years later Oglethorpe sailed beyond the loosely held border breached three decades earlier by James Moore. England claimed additional territory as far south as the mouth of the St. Johns River.

The change we celebrate occurred in 1736 when Santa Maria Island was re-named Amelia in honor of Amelia Sophia Eleanora, the 25-year old daughter of George II. In a letter to the Duke of Newcastle, Oglethorpe wrote: " The next island, the fairest of this province, I called Amelia. Oranges, myrtles and vines grow wild upon it." Our namesake led a life of privilege at court, but kept a sad secret until her dying day. A locket found around her neck held a likeness of the Crown Prince of Prussia, the future Frederick the Great. They had been betrothed, but Frederick's father had changed his mind and chosen a bride whose lineage was more powerful and suitable than that of the Hanoverian Princess. While Frederick would marry, Amelia remained single for the rest of her life. And what a life! She loved to drink and gamble. She enjoyed the company of men, and developed a sharp tongue and a quick wit. Amelia's final resting-place is the Henry VII Chapel in London's Westminster Abbey.

Not content to just name the island, Oglethorpe established a small fort on the bluff in Old Town. This served to further protect the disputed borders of Georgia. England held the island until 1742, at which point Amelia Island was unoccupied by either her English or Spanish claimants. Who would reign supreme? The Seven Years' War, or as it is known in America, the French and Indian War, proved decisive in the struggle to hold the island and establish which of the contenders' flags would be next.

As a result of the Treaty of Paris which ended the French and Indian War in **1763**, the **THIRD FLAG**, that of **ENGLAND**, officially flew over our island for the next twenty years. Spain kept its presence in Cuba in exchange for giving up La Florida. The second Earl of Egmont, John Perceval, was granted a plantation of 10,000 acres on Amelia Island. His name may have briefly supplanted Amelia's as the island's moniker. Through the successful management of Stephen Egan, Egmont and his heirs profited by raising indigo and turning it into a rich, blue dye. Indigofera tinctoria, a member of the pea family, grows wild on the island today. Once added to a colorless tea of water-steeped indigo plant materials, a secret ingredient was found that triggered the oxygenation process creating the blue color. It also enhanced the alkalinity necessary to make the dye soluble and able to adhere to cloth. Excess liquid was poured off the accumulated sludge. Brick-shaped blocks were then formed and allowed to dry. The "secret ingredient?": urine! Imagine the scent that wafted over the island when indigo production was at its peak.

The British now controlled the entire coastline of North America. Their Empire was expanding rapidly as they consolidated their hold. In order to catalogue and discover the natural treasures, men of science turned their attention to this new land. William Bartram, whose father had been the Royal Horticulturist to George I, visited Amelia Island in 1774. Among other things, he observed "a spacious forest of live oaks and palms; a creek running through a narrow salt marsh and large Indian tumuli where their bones are entombed in these heaps of earth and shells."

England learned from the difficulties faced by Spain in attempting to control the vast reaches of La Florida. The British divided the territory into two separate entities, East and West Florida. In reality, they had created two new colonies in addition to the original thirteen. Patrick Tonyn, Governor of East Florida, was responsible for encouraging many thousands of British settlers to apply for land grants. They introduced the system of plantations supported by slave labor that had proven so successful elsewhere in the South. An age of prosperity was about to emerge just as the Revolutionary War began.

Amelia Island was a casualty of this war in 1777, when a detachment of Col. Samuel Elbert's Continentals burned all of the homes on the island. In an incident that preceded the fire, one of his men had been killed after an island resident had fled to the mainland to bring back British support. The fire was Elbert's retaliation. Once again, the island was uninhabited until the arrival of a small but determined family.

Patrick Tonyn offered a land grant on the deserted bluff to the English widow, Mary Mattair. In the spring of 1783 she arrived with her two children, Maria and Luis. This was the same year a second Treaty of Paris was drafted, ending the Revolutionary War. In addition to granting independence to the original thirteen colonies, England was forced to relinquish Florida, which was returned to Spain. The Second Spanish Period had begun.

After the treaty had been ratified, the bluff, the harbor and the island were no longer deserted. Panic-stricken refugees flooded the area. With its harbor, Amelia Island became the major port of embarkation for the English Protestants as they fled the feared iron hand and dreaded Catholicism of their new Spanish masters. The dock and warehouses held slaves, recently harvested crops and even plantation houses that had been taken down board by board and numbered to facilitate rebuilding in a safer territory. Everything and everybody had to be ready to board the next ship setting sail from Amelia's harbor.

The evacuees were unaware that Spain had learned a

vital lesson: colonists were needed if they were to succeed in holding La Florida. Spain chose to honor existing land grants and to avoid the religious issue. The only thing required was an oath of allegiance to the Spanish crown. Mary Mattair and her two children had no wealth to protect, and nothing to lose. They took the oath, only to survive and prosper in their new home, while thousands of colonists fled toward uncertain futures. The Mattair's small plot of land on the bluff was the location chosen for a fortification designed to protect the harbor. Spain wanted to guarantee that they would never again lose control of La Florida's northeastern border. Who was the wise man who said, "never say never?" The original Mattair grant was taken in exchange for property elsewhere on the island and the mainland. A dynasty that would benefit present-day Fernandina Beach had been founded.

Domingo Fernandez came to Amelia Island in 1790. In addition to receiving a land grant, he was appointed to the position of harbor pilot. He and Maria Mattair, who was by now an orphan, were married two days before Christmas in 1793. During this same period, families like that of Samuel and Isabel McQueen Harrison arrived on the island to establish plantations. Little did the Harrisons know that their home would rise above the dual site of two missions that were discussed earlier, Santa Maria de Yamassee and the Doctrina of Santa Catalina de Guale. When anything "new" is done on an island as ancient as Amelia, it is nearly impossible to do it without layering over earlier, perhaps forgotten accomplishments. From this perspective, one could view the entire island as a metaphor of one enormous midden. Layer upon layer of history awaits exploration and interpretation.

Following the Napoleonic Wars, another European confrontation brought destruction to the island. In March of 1793 France declared war against Spain. The original contenders for the island had yet to resolve their conflicting territorial claims. Fearing that the island could easily fall prey to the French, Governor Quesada ordered an evacuation, with all useful buildings to be put to the torch. In 1795 the residents, including Domingo and Maria Mattair- Fernandez, followed the governor's orders shortly before the French tricolor entered our harbor on the mast of the French warship Las Casas. A treaty ending hostilities was signed in August of that year. Once again, Amelia Island would have to rise from her ashes.

On the international front, the British Royal Navy enacted a policy that enraged the Americans. British-born American citizens were being impressed, or kidnapped and involuntarily forced into the service of the Royal Navy. The prevailing British wisdom held that if you were born a British subject, you remained one for the rest of your life. Whether they wanted to or not, English subjects were required to serve in the Crown's understaffed Navy. While at sea, American citizens of British birth were at grave peril.

In an attempt to avert war and to call a halt to the British impressment policy, Thomas Jefferson convinced Congress to adopt the Embargo Act in 1807. While effectively closing off European trade, it played havoc with our new national economy. However, this would prove a boon to Amelia Island. The United States and its Embargo ended where the U.S. ended, at the southern border of Georgia. Since the island was still a territory of Spain, our harbor became the "back door" into the United States! The following year marked the passage of the U.S. Slave Importation Prohibition. New shipments were not allowed to enter U.S. ports, but slaves already in place could be bought and sold as before. Again, Amelia Island and our harbor offered a "back door" into the U.S., with untold opportunities for gaining wealth from illegal trade practices. The bluff and our harbor were seething with activity.

One of the many men of achievement to choose Amelia Island as their home during these exciting years was George Clarke. He served as Lieutenant Governor of Spanish East Florida and as the Surveyor General. It was his design that helped to bring order to the bluff. In 1811, through his expertise, Fernandina became the last town platted by Spain in the Western Hemisphere. To give you some perspective on who the islanders were, just two years later the official census counted well over half of the population of 1,330 as being black. Most of these were on outlying plantations, but 37 of the 41 free blacks and mulattoes actually lived in the town. By order of Governor Enrique White, the newly organized town was named for the current Bourbon monarch of Spain, Ferdinand VII. His was a dubious reign, for among his accomplishments was the revival of the Inquisition.

While a sense of physical order had been imposed on the town, it was still the scene of illicit trading that continued to undermine the U.S. economy. Politicians lacked the vital key they needed to lock the "back door". An alarming number of British ships were starting to gather in Fernandina's harbor. With Canada already in British hands, there was a perceived threat that the United States was about to be attacked on two fronts. Britain, still smarting from her defeat in the Revolutionary War, could use her combined forces in Florida and Canada to mount a simultaneous offensive, north and south. The U.S. would then be caught in a potentially lethal vise. But Amelia Island was Spanish, not British! This fact led

President Madison to call a secret session of Congress in 1811. The measure that was passed allowed the President to spend $100,000 and to use the Army and Navy to "expel by force any foreign power threatening Spanish Florida." The English presence in Fernandina's harbor was definitely perceived as being "threatening!"

Rather than mount a massive military action, President Madison thought it prudent to encourage people from the area, local patriots, to declare their independence from foreign powers and to request that they be brought under the protection of the U.S. flag. In essence, they would create a rebellion of patriots of the United States of America. The perfect man to lead the rebellion was already on the scene. President Madison chose General George Mathews, a 72-year old Revolutionary War hero and former Governor of Georgia. Plantation owners from Florida and Georgia, like John Houstoun McIntosh, were enlisted in the effort.

The Patriots ultimately took over the island, and the **FOURTH FLAG**, that of the **PATRIOTS**, flew over Fernandina's Plaza on **March 17, 1812**. Twenty-four hours later the island was ceded to the United States of America by the rebels. The design of the flag shows the silhouette of an advancing, armed soldier underlined by the motto Salus Populi lex Suprema, meaning, "the well being of the people is the supreme law." This initiative would eventually destroy the lives of several leading figures of the rebellion and force our own country to back down in deference to Spain. Madison decided not to stand behind the actions he had authorized. We were about to enter the War of 1812 with England, and we did not have the resources to fight Spain at the same time.

Once the patriots left, Spain was even more determined that Amelia Island and La Florida should be adequately protected from forces beyond the border. The centuries' old tradition of using missions to secure territories had been supplanted by creating fortifications. Beginning in 1816, Fort San Carlos was built on the Plaza and armed with a battery of 10 guns. It was a case of too little, too late. Within the span of 4 years, 3 of our 8 flags rose in quick succession.

The next threat on the horizon came not from the direction of Europe, but from South America. General Gregor MacGregor had set his sights on aiding the cause of General Simon Bolivar in the struggle for Venezuelan independence from Spain. When the goal was nearly achieved, MacGregor was asked to leave. After all, who would credit a Scottish hero of Latin American independence? MacGregor's next destination was North America, where La Florida's struggles had captured his imagination and fueled his ambition for a country of his own. From Philadelphia and Baltimore, to Charleston and Savannah, he attempted to raise the necessary support. Many promises were made, but in reality he had little money and a force of only 55 American soldiers to mount the anticipated coup. Aware of Spain's deficiencies, as well as his own, he sent a spy ahead to Amelia Island to spread a rumor that a massive force of 1,000 professional men-at-arms was on its way. Meanwhile, back at the recently completed Fort San Carlos, Commandant Francisco Morales had fewer than 60 tired, battle-weary men at his command. MacGregor anchored his ship out of sight from the fort, coercing a local fisherman to sail ahead to warn Morales of impending doom.

For those of you who don't believe that something as innocent as a weed can change the course of history, the following should be of interest. An unbearably hot day had dawned on June 29th, 1817. With MacGregor's men now on shore, the mosquitoes and gnats were brutal. In agony, the men advanced toward the woods behind the present-day location of Fort Clinch State Park, where they discovered a patch of dog fennel. This plume-like weed, which is a natural insect repellant, grows wild on the island. The men picked sprigs and stuck them in their helmets. The march continued until reaching the marsh and creek that separated them from Fort San Carlos. Morales caught sight of the men, advancing in twos and threes, plumes held high. He felt sure he was seeing the advance guard! At any moment 1,000 men would come charging from the forest to slaughter all who resisted. MacGregor's handful of men, dog fennel and all, faced Morales and took the fort without a single shot being fired! The flag of Spain was lowered, and our **FIFTH FLAG**, that of **THE GREEN CROSS OF FLORIDA**, was raised on **June 29, 1817**. It was MacGregor's family flag, a St. George's green cross on a field of white.

MacGregor was fast running out of money and enthusiasm for what he perceived to be a losing proposition. By the beginning of September, Gregor MacGregor, his wife and a few loyal men set sail to continue their search for a country they could call their own. Left behind were a handful of men, including Jared Irwin, a former U.S. congressman from Pennsylvania and Ruggles Hubbard, a former High Sheriff from New York. These determined few sought to maintain their possession of Amelia Island in spite of Spanish opposition. The two forces confronted one another at the Battle of McClure's Hill. By driving north on 14th Street toward Old Town, as you reach the crest of a slight rise, you pass a State marker commemorating the battle. In an effort to regain control, the Spanish devised a two-pronged attack. Gunboats would fire on the town from the harbor, while a force on McClure's Hill would fire from the land. The intention was to catch Fernandina between the crossfire of two positions, thereby destroying the rebels' resistance. Irwin and the Spanish in the harbor were evenly matched and fought without casualties. Late in the day Irwin fired on McClure's Hill, over-shooting the target. The shots landed behind the hill, where the Spanish force had camped. There were injuries, and two Spaniards were killed. Chaos ensued as the land based forces retreated. Irwin had won the battle by missing his intended target!

Amelia Island was just days away from yet another conquest. In mid September the privateer, Luis Aury, sailed into the harbor. The line between being called a privateer or a pirate is slim but clearly defined. A privateer performs his actions under the authorization of a political entity, rather than at his own whim. The revolutionary Republic of Mexico had sanctioned Aury in the course of their struggle for freedom from Spain's domination. Seeking better opportunities in a port still within Spain's troubled territories, Aury sailed from his previous base of operations in Galveston, Texas. Before beginning the eastward journey, surviving members of Jean Lafitte's band of pirates joined his crew. The island's remaining inhabitants, including what was left of Irwin and Hubbard's men, were not prepared to defend Amelia Island from international bandits. Our **SIXTH FLAG**, that of the **MEXICAN REVOLUTIONARIES**, was raised on **September 21st, 1817**.

John Houstoun McIntosh, former leader of the Patriots Rebellion, immediately alerted Washington. The 1811 Secret Act of Congress was about to reap further benefits. In spite of current diplomatic negotiations in which Spain was being encouraged to relinquish her claim on La Florida in favor of America, President James Monroe authorized the use of force. Diplomatic arguments ensued between the Federal Government and Aury's recently created political entity, the Republic of Amelia. Backed by the arrival of Federal troops and ships, the flag of the United States ended Aury's claim and his Republic on December 23, 1817. Once again, the U.S. held the island "in trust for Spain."

Fate was not dealing Spain a winning hand. The effects of a weakening political climate in Spain were added to mounting debts inflated by claims from U.S. citizens along the Georgia/Florida border. The U.S. offered further territorial threats with the Louisiana Purchase in 1803. Spain appeared to be at risk of being pushed from the North American continent. The recent embarrassment caused by the Federal Government seizing Amelia Island for the second time was intensified by General Andrew Jackson's sweep across the Florida border to

deal with the Seminole Indians. Spain seemed powerless. On **July 10, 1821** our **SEVENTH FLAG**, that of **THE UNITED STATES OF AMERICA**, would fly not only over our harbor, but also over all of what had once been La Florida. In exchange for excusing massive debts, Florida became a territory of the U.S.

Surely, the parade of flags had finally ended. The small bluff-top town evolved from a neatly aligned collection of 40 frame structures to become the inspiration for a dream of global dimensions. In 1824 Fernandina was declared the county seat of recently created Nassau County. The Federal Government sponsored projects that included a seawall to protect the bluff and a two-storied structure on the Plaza. Land for a lighthouse was purchased from Maria Mattair-Fernandez. Formerly on Cumberland Island, the lighthouse was moved to Amelia, brick by brick, spiraling granite step by step, and reconstructed on its new site in 1839. The beacon sends out a beam of light that still pierces the night sky many miles out to the open ocean. It is the farthest inland of any in our system of coastal lighthouses. Land was also acquired for the eventual construction of Fort Clinch. This barrier island was destined for an important future, and no one saw this more clearly than one man, David Levy Yulee.

No tale of nineteenth century Amelia Island or Florida is complete without the mention of this unique man of vision who began life with one name, David Levy, and ended it with another, David Levy Yulee. He was of Sephardic Jewish heritage. One of four children, David was born June 12, 1810, in Charlotte Amalie on the West Indies' island of St. Thomas. Shortly thereafter his parents separated. His father, Moses Levy, moved to Cuba and eventually to the United States. At the same time, rumors were circulating that La Florida might soon become a territory. By purchasing land, Moses and his sons would be granted citizenship. Travelling first to Philadelphia and then to La Florida, he began purchasing large parcels of land that would eventually include the Arredondo Grant, the single largest Spanish land grant in La Florida.

Moses brought his two sons, David and Elias, first to Cuba and then to the United States, where they were sent to further their education. David went to the Norfolk Academy, Elias to Harvard. The boys' formal education ended in 1827, when Moses withdrew financial support. Penniless, the boys returned to the Territory of Florida, where David continued his education under the guidance of the overseer of his father's Micanopy plantation. During the next five years, David came to realize that his best opportunities lay in the political and legal arenas. To this end, he studied the law with Robert

Raymond Reid, who later became the Territorial Governor of Florida.

After serving on the St. Joseph's Convention, which drafted our state constitution, David was elected as the Democratic Territorial Delegate for the first of two terms. His move to Washington, D.C. in 1841 marked an expansion of his sphere of influence from regional to national. While in Washington he met the love of his life, Nannie Wickliffe, daughter of the former governor of Kentucky and Postmaster General under President John Tyler.

David achieved one of his objectives on March 3, 1845, when President Tyler signed the bill admitting Florida as the 27th state. In recognition of his devotion to the cause, David became known as the "Father of Florida Statehood." Further honors followed, including his appointment as one of the two first senators representing the newly formed state of Florida in Washington, D.C. David Levy became the first Jew to serve his country on the national level in the Senate.

On April 7, 1846, David and Nannie were married. The previous year he had gone before the Florida Assembly to petition to have the surname Yulee added to his name. The inspiration was from his grandfather, Jacoub Ben Youle, a man with a colorful history of his own. At this time David began acquiring property near the mouth of the Homosassa River and in Archer, Florida. The Yulee family would prosper over the years and grow to include four children.

Defeated in his bid for a second term in the Senate, David Levy Yulee focused his boundless energy on a dream that had never been far from his heart. The lessons of History informed him that ships from Europe and the North American coastal ports could easily enter Amelia Island's harbor. He envisioned spanning the East and West coasts of Florida with a rail line carved through the terrirtory's sparsely inhabited interior. The Gulf of Mexico gave access to the Mississippi River Delta, ultimately opening river ports as far as the Great Lakes region. David was following the ancient trade routes of the Timucuans. If a second short rail line were constructed across the isthmus of Mexico, which fronted on the Gulf, Pacific ports and vast markets in the Orient could also be included. The vision of a worldwide trade network could be realized with only two comparatively short rail lines. The first trans-peninsular Florida railroad was about to be created.

David had the contacts and the expertise to have the railroad constructed. But there was one thing he did not have: land on Amelia Island. Old Town was not suitable due to the high bluff access to the harbor and the surrounding marshland. His dilemma was resolved by decisive action. An ironclad will protected the vast estates of Maria Mattair-Fernandez. One parcel fronting on the harbor offered the ideal location. As a lawyer admitted to practice in all of Florida's courts, David sued and was successful in convincing a judge to allow the heirs to sell the land to two businessmen, who had agreed, in turn, to sell it to David. The Yellow Bluff Plantation, the Eliza or Louisa Plantation and other parcels of land would ultimately come to David for $9,141.94.

After much discussion Cedar Key, with a similar harbor on the West Coast, was chosen as the Gulf terminus. In 1853 the government of Mexico committed to building their portion over the isthmus. Construction of the Florida span began in 1855, the same year that David Levy Yulee was appointed U.S. Senator for his second and final term. He used his time in Washington to good purpose, being instrumental in the passage of the Federal Land Grant Bill, which brought 500,000 additional acres to his railroad. As Chairman of the Naval Affairs Committee, he saw to it that the shoals were removed from the Amelia River. As Chairman of the Post Office and Post Roads Committee, he had the as yet to be completed railroad awarded the contract for mail delivery. The massive investment of capital necessary to keep the project moving forward was supported by issuing bonds, mortgaging personal property that included slaves and even, in 1858, by encouraging investments from the North. This pattern continued through the years.

While the 155.5-mile long railroad was nearing completion, construction continued in Fernandina. The official Platt of the city was issued in 1857. It included Old Town, but the focus was shifted to a more accessible area of the harbor. The wide dividing street in the middle that stretched from the harbor to the Atlantic Ocean was named **Centre Street**. The town was laid out in a grid pattern with intersecting sequentially numbered streets, **Front Street** being the first, then **2nd Street**, **3rd Street** and so on. The crossing streets, north and south, were alphabetical. Side streets on the south progressed from **A**sh, to **B**eech to **C**edar, and so on, with names representing Nature's bounty on the island. Side streets on the north began with **A**lachua, then **B**roome, then **C**alhoun, and so on, listing the counties of Florida. Broome Street was the exception, as it had been named for the governor who signed the charter for the railroad. Homes, churches, hotels and dockside structures began to appear. By 1859 there were ships from Savannah and Charleston on a daily basis. Given the grid layout of Fernandina's streets, the presence of a "Central Park" on the original Platt, and Amelia Island's size of 11,600 acres, these statistics should remind you of another island with a similar trade and tourist based economy located slightly to the north of us. If you thought of Manhattan, you are correct.

When the telegraph arrived in 1860, David sent the following message to the President of New York's Chamber of Commerce: "Fernandina, a new seaport in the South, presents herself, through your Chamber, for recognition in the commercial circles of the world." A note he wrote on a copy of the telegram predicts, "Thirty years hence it (Fernandina) will be one of the three leading ports of the South."

But tensions were mounting in Washington as the buildup of grievances between the North and the South became intolerable. On January 11, 1861 Florida seceded from the Union. Ten days later, David was at the head of the Southern delegation as it left. A letter he wrote while still sitting as Florida's senator encouraged seizing Federal arms and fortifications. At War's end this letter would be responsible for ten long months of imprisonment. His statements, by their timing, were considered to be evidence of treason.

Back home in Fernandina, there was excitement of a different kind. On March 1, 1861 the first train left Fernandina and arrived in Cedar Key. The first half of David's dream of a worldwide trade network had been realized! A month later the future of the railroad, as well as that of the country, would face a devastating challenge. The second half of the dream, the Mexican line, fell victim to the events that followed. On **April 12, 1861** the Battle of Ft. Sumter began the Civil War. Our **EIGHTH FLAG**, that of the **CONFEDERACY**, was flown over the island.

The flag of the United States of America returned to Amelia Island on March 3, 1862. David Levy Yulee barely managed to escape on the last train to leave the island. Retreating Confederate troops destroyed sections of the track, since it was money David secured from the North that had seen to its completion.

With the end of the war in 1865, most of the troops left, while the First New York Engineers and the 7th Infantry were put in place for the duration of the Reconstruction. As a result of the new voting laws they helped to enforce, the first election in the South to include both black and white male voters was held in Fernandina. A white candidate won, though in later years numerous black public officials were elected. In the meantime, men who had served on the island during the war returned. They brought their families and started prosperous businesses. However, in 1876 we barely survived the first of three devastating fires in our downtown. Once the rebuilding had taken place, we were well into our first "Golden Age." The Mallory Company steamship line was making weekly trips to our harbor, bringing wealthy visitors to experience our gentle climate, pristine beaches and luxurious hotels. Among the guests was President Ulysses S. Grant who, as a general at the close of the Civil War, was responsible for having David Levy Yulee released after his ten months imprisonment in Fort Pulaski, Georgia. The decade of the 1880s brought an architect, Robert Sands Schuyler, a former Union cavalryman. Many of the fine homes and the church he designed are still standing. Subsequent fires swept away part of the business district and residential area in 1883, but a lesson had been learned. Masonry construction was mandated for all replacement commercial structures. This decision has given Fernandina's business district the Italianate Victorian style that enchants visitors and residents alike in the twenty-first century. In 1888 an epidemic of yellow fever suspended the island's growth. Throughout our early history, the threat of disease always lurked beneath the best of times.

By the late 1890s our port was the hub for contraband arms supplying the rebel Cuban forces. While completing negotiations for armaments, Jose Marti was a guest at the Florida House, which still welcomes island visitors. In 1898 preparations for the Spanish American War brought 10,000 troops to Ft. Clinch and the area. This was also the year of our most devastating hurricane on record. It caused destruction, but it also brought a man of Sicilian heritage to our shores. Sollecito "Mike" Salvador was an immigrant whose skill and ingenuity lead to our island being called the "birthplace of the modern shrimping industry" in the early twentieth century.

From the end of one century to the beginning of the next, the competing railroad empires of Flagler and Plant combined to shift the focus of commercial opportunities and tourism to other parts of the state. Some aspects of the regional economy suffered as the promise of a bright future seemed to be slipping further from our grasp. It was not until the late 1930s that a sustaining industry came to the island. The Container Corporation, today known as Smurfit-Stone Corporation, built a plant between "new" Fernandina and Old Town. Rayonier Corporation constructed a pulp mill. Both industries continue to contribute to the quality of life in our area. This would also be the decade in which the Afro-American Life Insurance Company established American Beach on the south end of the island in 1935. It is one of the few remaining beach resorts created by and for African-Americans. Its unique story is the subject of several recently published books and media events.

Through a voter referendum and a special act of the legislature in 1951, an adaptation of our former name evolved that both honored our history and looked toward the future. If David Levy Yulee could change his name and create a railroad, surely we could change our name and create a second "Golden Age!" Fernandina became Fernandina Beach. The evolution of the town's name serves as a constant reminder that our history, as well as our location on a barrier island, combine to define our unique identity.

In the 1970s concerned residents formed the Amelia Island Fernandina Restoration Foundation to nurture the development of our Historic District which, along with several individual buildings, is listed in the National Register of Historic Places. By ordinance, the city of Fernandina Beach created the Historic District Council (HDC) to review new construction and renovation efforts within the Historic District. Today, the preservation spirit remains strong in our community, as seen by projects ranging from Trinity United Methodist Church and St. Michael's Academy, to Peck Center and numerous restorations undertaken by local homeowners and businessmen. Many visitors are surprised to learn that Florida holds an unusual distinction. The on-going commitment of state funds to preserving the built environment is unmatched by any other state in the Union. This has, in turn, inspired new construction that enhances and supports the historic structures.

The first major new construction project on the island's south end was the Amelia Island Plantation, which offers both residential and resort options in a setting of rare beauty. Union Carbide had decided to sell off its no longer profitable Titanium mining holdings to an imaginative developer on Hilton Head Island, Charles Fraser. From its creation in the 1970s it has maintained stringent environmental controls that have placed all of the amenities you can imagine beneath a natural canopy of trees. Were he able to return for a brief look, Jean Ribault, the first recorded "foreign" visitor who brought the flag of France with him, could gaze across the Plantation and see a familiar landscape. Later developments included the Ritz-Carlton, Amelia Island, which was completed in 1991. World-class accommodations meet and exceed the expectations of the most discriminating visitors. Island guests have a wide range of choices, from Bed and Breakfast Inns scattered throughout the Historic District and along the Atlantic Coast, to the convenience and luxury of Summer Beach and family-friendly motels. The twenty-first century brought the Hampton Inn & Suites ~ Amelia Island, "Historic Harbor Front Hotel," to the heart of downtown Fernandina Beach.

Once you have left the mainland, Amelia Island entices you to linger. Elegant restaurants and unique shops and galleries hold the promise of endless discoveries. With championship public and private golf courses and tennis facilities, an airport and moorings for private vessels, there is something for everyone. Fort Clinch State Park encourages your adventurous spirit. If fishing, kayaking, birding or bicycling is your pleasure, you will find abundant opportunities. From a sunrise walk along an unspoiled, shimmering stretch of beach, to a horseback ride following the ever-shifting strip where the sea and sand meet, Amelia Island encourages you to explore your fantasies.

The award-winning Amelia Island Museum of History, founded in 1986, is committed to helping you make the most of your visit to the island. Our mission is simple: education with pleasure. Our method is direct: docents tell you our regional story steeped in the ancient traditions of the storyteller. Monday through Saturday, you can take either of the twice-daily Eight-Flag Exhibit Hall Tours at our headquarters in the historic former Nassau County Jailhouse. We are located on the corner of Cedar and 3rd Streets, a three-block stroll from downtown Fernandina Beach. You can also arrange walking and driving tours of the Historic District, the island and county. Lectures and events, including a popular series of Elderhostel programs, are available by booking in advance. On-site re-enactors allow you to meet historical personalities from Nassau County's past. David Levy Yulee and Maria Mattair-Fernandez await the pleasure of your company at the Amelia Island Museum of History.

Now that you have had a chance to familiarize yourself with the island's eight-flag history, Roger and I extend a personal invitation for you to begin your visual journey. The photographs that follow are meant to inspire you. The photographer and the author cherish the magical land they are fortunate enough to call home. We welcome the opportunity to share it with you.

THE END…
Or better yet…

THE BEGINNING…

Of the next unwritten chapter,
Your chapter, in the continuing story of Amelia Island!

Ocean, Beach & Dunes

Chapter II

The same Brown Pelican reflects on his universe of sky, sea and sand. He is inviting you to share it.

Waves of wind and water sculpt the dunes.
Fragile roots of sea oats (Uniola poniculata)
attempt to hold back the tide of change. Man-
made barriers join the struggle for permanence,
but the ultimate victory belongs to nature.

Caught before the next foot falls: little man,
big shadow. The sand and sea of Amelia
Island have the power to rekindle our sense
of wonder.

Channel markers help to guide ships safely through our complex water channels. Low tide reveals all, as families head to the water's edge to discover treasures dredged from the ocean's depth. INSET: A closer look shows Incongruous Ark Shells (Anadara brasiliana), a cylindrical Lettered Olive (Oliva sayana) in the upper left corner, and the ultimate bounty, a 6 to 10 million year old fossilized tooth of the extinct Giant White Shark (Carcharodon megalodon).

A rare moment in time when man and birds, sun and sand, all become one with the life-sustaining sea. (below left)

Waves of Sanderlings (Calidris alba) in their winter plumage strut along sea-slick shores, their shadows and reflected images accompanying their quest for sustenance. (below right)

The cry of the gulls, the crash of the waves...Nature's music inspires serenity.

Watch the sun rise from your room at the elegant Elizabeth Pointe Lodge, an oceanfront B&B on the island's north end. INSET: For centuries, islanders have prospered by harvesting the ocean's bounty.

Ocean view, oceanfront: homeowners have staked their claims on both sides of Fletcher Avenue as it follows miles of glistening Allegheny Mountain quartz beaches. Both the City of Fernandina Beach and Nassau County have provided numerous public access areas for residents and visitors alike to share this natural wonder.

Some island residents, like the Gopher Tortoise (Gopherus polyphemus), carry their homes on their backs! The sea species nesting sites are protected, and an active turtle-watch monitors their progress from laying of eggs to return of hatchlings to their world of water.

Sandy shores and warm temperatures nurture a coastal ecology that includes a variety of cacti, including the Prickly-pear Cactus (Opuntia humifusa). Yellow blossoms, which last only a short while, capture and hold the wonder of the summer sun.

Centre Street, North

Chapter III

Our Brown Pelican looks up Front Street before choosing his "north" wing for a closer inspection and a bit of grooming attention. Let's follow his lead.

The original grid system of the Platt from 1857 still defines the Historic District and beyond. David Levy Yulee's plan for the future is apparent with the vast harbor, and as glimpsed in the upper left hand corner, the presence of a train in close proximity to the harbor. The "Christopher Wren" cupola of the County Courthouse on Centre Street, to the left, marks the building height restriction currently in place.

Centre Street was a broad, straight thoroughfare until it was restructured in the 1970s. Original sections of six-sided pavers were preserved, and bricks that covered the road surface were reused at cross walks. Angled parking, trees and seasonal plantings soften the look of our Italianate Victorian Seaport City. Comfortable benches encourage conversation and reflection, or a respite from the temptations of nearby specialty and antique shops.

Northeast Florida's oldest continuously operating bar, the Palace Saloon, was built in 1878 as a men's haberdashery emporium. Once, countless bars serviced the desires of ordinary seamen, but this one was created to cater to the "gold braid trade" of the ships' officers and the local aristocracy, like the Carnegie family of nearby Cumberland Island.

The Greek Revival style First Presbyterian Church has occupied this site on the first block of North 6th Street since 1859. It is the oldest of all the remaining church structures on the island. David Levy Yulee's wife, Nannie, was one of the original members, while the first minister, Archibald Baker, became a close family friend of the Yulees. Throughout the island, Sabal Palms (Sabal palmetto), accent the landscape.

The 1886 Hirth House, designed by New York architect Robert Sands Schuyler, marks the second block of North 6th Street, known as the "Silk Stocking" District. (If you could afford silk stockings, you could afford to live in this neighborhood!) Descendants of the original builders still occupy many of the homes on this block. Louis G. Hirth arrived in America from Germany without prospects. He would become one of Fernandina's leading citizens, opening the Palace Saloon in 1903.

The Josiah Prescott House in the "Silk Stocking" District, circa 1876. Prescott was the builder of the men's haberdashery shop that would years later be turned into the Palace Saloon by one of his neighbors, Louis Hirth.

Built for prominent local physician Dr. D. G. Humphreys between 1900 and 1902, this "Silk Stocking" District home inspired a "copycat" house built by his partner, Dr. Horsey, on Centre Street between 6th and 7th Streets.

The Liberty Billings House on North 5th Street sits across from the St. Michael's Church block. Records indicate that it was built in 1883, though an earlier date is possible.

Our Centre Street Post Office, circa 1912, replicates the de Medici Palazzo in Florence, Italy. It is in the Italian Renaissance Revival style. Those of you who have read the History Chapter will know why this allusion to Catherine de Medici has a special meaning to residents of Florida's First Coast.

A North 4th Street success story: local citizens saved this once derelict structure. It has been returned to its original purpose, welcoming the 21st century as a private home. The historic marker is one of many throughout the island, delighting visitors with the opportunity to explore and learn on their own.

St. Michael's Catholic Church at the corner of North 4th and Broome Streets was the town's first brick building, completed in 1872. Surrounded by late 19th and early 20th century homes, it shares the block with the Fernandez Reserve, the family burial plot of the original owners of the land upon which present-day Fernandina Beach was founded. The recently restored St. Michael's Academy, a private school, completes the compound.

A house that love built, the Spanish Colonial Revival style Villa Las Palmas, is located at the corner of North 4th and Alachua Streets. It was constructed in 1910 by Nathaniel B. Borden, lumberman and Cuban consul, for his beautiful and much younger wife, Flossie. The adjacent vacant lot at the corner of North 3rd and Alachua Streets was the original site of David Levy Yulee's now demolished home. In recognition of the contributions of Yulee and others, The Jewish History Trail includes sites on the island.

The Amelia Island Lighthouse is the furthermost inland of our coastal lighthouses. First constructed on Cumberland Island in 1820, it was later moved, brick by brick, spiraling granite step by step, to Amelia Island in 1839. Located in a residential district, it constitutes a separate historic district within the city limits. As the oldest, still operational lighthouse in Florida, this landmark has been turned over to the city.

Ft. Clinch, on the North end of the island, was begun in 1847, just two years after Florida became the 27th State. After the first year of the Civil War, the Union seized it in what was the largest amphibious attack yet launched by our young federal government. Ft. Clinch State Park offers picnicking, camping, swimming, saltwater fishing and boating, as well as Union re-enactors at the fort.

It is easy to appreciate how the Governor Mouton Camellia (Camellia japonica) and other members of this colorful family have inspired poets, musicians and dreamers. Island-born Gustav George Gerbing so fell under their spell that he created the Gerbing Camellia and Azalea Gardens on 15 acres on the banks of the Amelia River. From 1932 to 1947, visitors came from throughout the country to watch the tide of color beginning with Camellias in late February and ending with the mid-March blooming Azaleas. While the formal gardens have disappeared, Gerbing's heritage is still evident in the ornamental plants that have survived.

Centre Street, South

Chapter IV

Our Brown Pelican is encouraging us to follow his example and to explore even more of the Historic District.

The restored Nassau County Courthouse on Centre Street, circa 1891, has been called "the finest surviving Victorian courthouse in Florida." With the exception of a comparatively brief period, Fernandina has been the seat of county government for one of the first counties organized in Florida.

Welcome to the Amelia Island Museum of History on the corner of 3rd and Cedar Streets. Originally a one-story jailhouse in 1878, the current Art Deco look evolved with the addition of a second story and more cells in the 1930s. Two decades later a wing was added in the back. Since 1986, in the ancient tradition of the storyteller, volunteers have been sharing the story of Amelia Island and Nassau County with residents and visitors alike.

Mid-block on 9th, between Centre and Ash Streets, First Missionary Baptist Church is home to one of Fernandina Beach's thriving African-American congregations. Built in 1874, its members have included Emma B. Delaney, the first black female missionary to Africa, and Capt. Neil Frink, the first African-American to become a licensed boat captain in the state. The Delaney sisters, descendants of the Fernandina Delaneys, were the inspiration for both a book and an award-winning Broadway play.

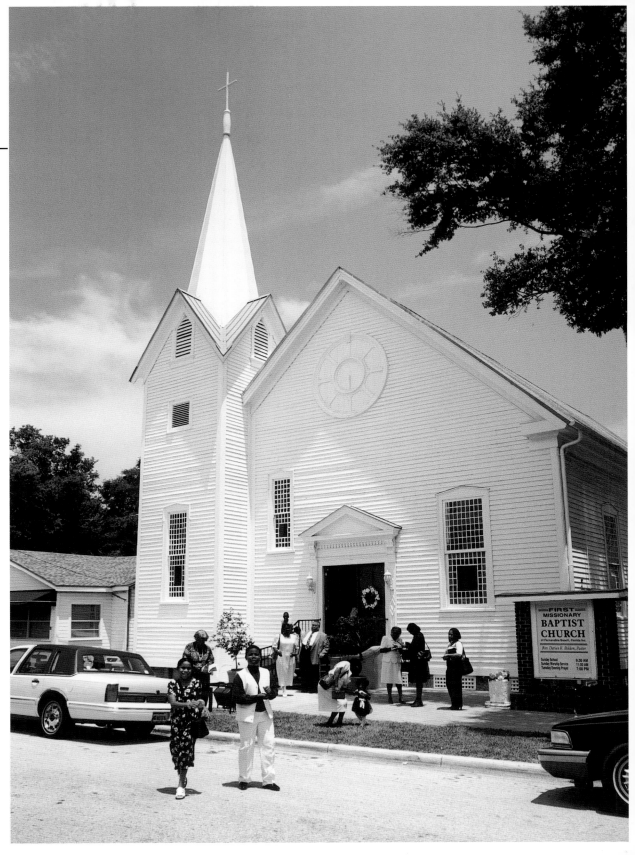

Colorful or muted, intimate or grand, new or old, our continually evolving architectural heritage celebrates the unique vision of each resident. This extends to the way in which we honor the holidays. Behind its picket fence, an island home sets the stage for a personalized view of the spiritual and secular joys of Easter.

The Florida House Inn continues a tradition of welcoming visitors that began when it was built by the Florida Railroad in 1857. Located on 3rd Street just one block off Centre Street, guests have ranged from Jose Marti, the "George Washington of Cuba," to the great stars of the Silent Film Era like Mary Pickford and Samuel Goldwyn. Family style meals lure hungry guests to sample "Florida Cracker" style cooking in Florida's oldest surviving tourist hotel.

The Italianate style Fairbanks House B & B, located on the corner of 7th and Cedar Streets, was built in 1885 for the extended family of George Rainsford Fairbanks. It was designed by Robert Sands Schuyler, former New York architect and direct descendant of one of George Washington's generals in the Revolutionary War. Fairbanks was the founder of the University of the South in Sewanee, Tennessee, and the editor and eventual owner of the Florida Mirror, which would become today's News-Leader, Florida's oldest weekly newspaper.

St. Peter's Episcopal Church, at the corner of 8th and Centre Streets, was the first building designed in Fernandina by Robert Sands Schuyler. Built of tabby, a mixture of sand, oyster shells, water and lime derived from burning shells, its Gothic Revival spire has pierced the skies of Fernandina since construction was completed in 1884. The shells were harvested from the island's ancient Timucuan middens. Their pipe organ is considered to be the earliest original installation in Florida.

The Lesesne House, circa 1861, is adjacent to the Post Office on Centre Street. Throughout its long history, it has remained a private residence. 450 of Fernandina Beach's historic structures were built before 1927, an impressive total for a small Florida community! The park-like setting brings an oasis of green to the heart of the Historic District.

The Williams House on the corner of Ash and 9th Streets was built in 1856. Purchased three years later by Marcellus Williams, a land surveyor and Florida pioneer, this home remained in the family for more than 100 years. Lush gardens and rooms filled with treasured antiques from the world's most exotic ports welcome guests to one of our premier B&Bs. Don't be surprised if one of Fernandina's resident ghosts decides to share your holiday adventure!

Fred W. Hoyt, a prosperous local banker and owner of a ship's chandlery, built the Hoyt House in 1905. Directly across the street from St. Peter's Episcopal Church, the park-like setting of Victorian plantings shaded by Live Oaks (Quercus virginiana) draped with Spanish moss (Tillandsia usneoides) invite guests to linger at this most hospitable B&B.

The Bailey House, at the corner of 7th and Ash Streets, stands as a monument to the love of Effingham Bailey for his wife, Kate. Listed on the National Register of Historic Places, this Queen Anne style home was designed by George Barber and built at the considerable cost of $10,000 in 1895. A wing was added in the late 20th century.

The Waas House, circa 1901, began life as a much smaller 1856 residence on the corner of Date and 7th Streets. Details like the Gothic Revival interpretation of the gable-end Palladian window were kept in place, while the later Queen Anne style veranda and tower were added by Dr. Waas. This architectural confection remains a private home.

The Addison House has occupied this corner of 7th and Ash Streets since 1876. When Christmas comes to Fernandina, residents celebrate the season.

Three decades ago the demolition of Centre Street's Keystone Hotel sparked the local preservation movement. Today, the Hampton Inn & Suites ~ Amelia Island, "Historic Harbor Front Hotel," welcomes guests to the first block of South 2nd Street, just off Centre Street. Victorian buildings in the Historic District inspired its traditional design. People from the island's past inspired the names of the conference rooms and suites, while Southern hospitality inspires the service. As you enter the lobby, lift your eyes from the antiques and let them come to rest on the ceiling. A surprise awaits you!

The Ash Street Inn on 7th Street was built as a gracious family home early in the twentieth century. The spacious veranda offers a stage where guests can linger, exchanging pleasantries with each other and passers-by. Our island welcome knows no season!

If eyes are the windows to the soul, then windows can perhaps be considered the pathway to the architectural spirit of a building. Trinity United Methodist Church was completed in 1893 and graced with an unusual suite of stained glass windows. While a tour sponsored by the Amelia Island Museum of History brought attention to the building, an island-wide support group, the Friends of Trinity, guided the award-winning restoration. This African-American church at the corner of Ash and 8th Streets serves as a model for the miracles that can be brought about through community preservation efforts.

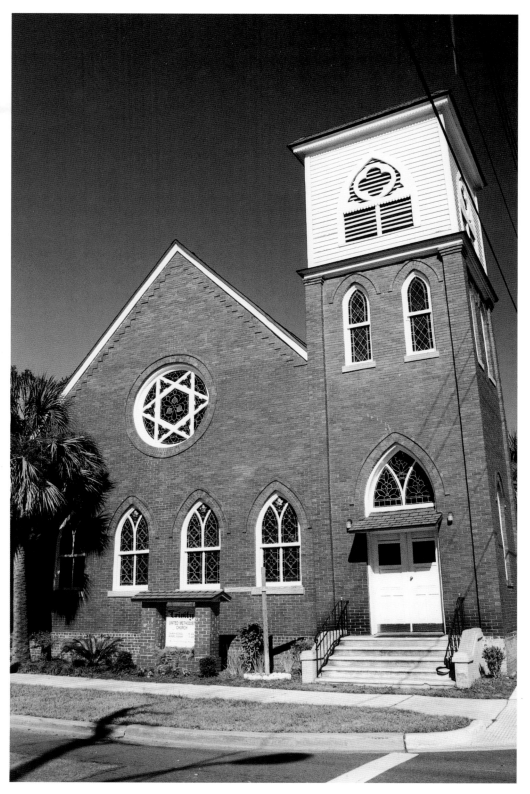

From pastel to primary, Formosa Azaleas (Rhododendrum indicum) lead an island-wide profusion of spring blossoms. Some of these relatives of the rhododendrons are descendants of Gus Gerbing's original plantings.

Island Events, Industry & Old Town

Chapter V

Our Brown Pelican seems to be encouraging us to gaze in yet another direction, lest we miss the diversity the island has to offer.

Mark your calendar and set your sights on The Isle of 8 Flags Shrimp Festival. Since 1964, the first weekend in May offers non-stop entertainment and family fun, from original artworks and world-class craft items and antiques, to fireworks and the Pirate Parade. More than 100,000 people come to share the good times…and the plentiful food offerings: especially the shrimp!

Decisions, decisions…look to the signs to guide you toward your next event. Everything is within easy walking distance in the downtown Historic District.

Young Spanish dancers perform for an enthusiastic Shrimp Festival audience during this multicultural weekend.

The Amelia Island Concours d'Elegance is one of the top three shows of its kind in the country. Founding sponsor Mercedes-Benz invites you to this yearly event, which can be savored at the host site, the Ritz-Carlton, Amelia Island. Each spring select greens and fairways of The Golf Club of Amelia Island showcase more than 200 unique automobiles. Seen here is a 1923 Mercedes Indy car.

A 1931 Cadillac V 12 Sport Phaeton is preparing to drive by an admiring audience.

This turn of the century Stanley Steamer Car shows that early motorists had to spend time in front of the wheel before they could get behind the wheel.

Two who flew, one who stayed. Our "star" Brown Pelican seems to be quite fond of his center stage position. This shot of the City Marina and its pleasure craft lured Roger down the ramp to get a better look at our patient pelican. His compatriots must have been camera-shy.

Present-day explorers, take note; the Marina offers you the opportunity to charter a boat for an excursion that will challenge the most ardent fishing enthusiast. Others might be looking to view the island and surrounding terrain as it was first seen by our eight flag bearers.

As the harbor sweeps northward, commercial fishing vessels frame the dock area where larger ships arrive. A recent visitor was the luxury liner, Silver Shadow, of the SilverSea Cruise Line.

From rowboats to sailboats to motor-powered vessels, shrimping emerged as a major local industry. While the geographic focus has shifted elsewhere, Fernandina is known as the birthplace of the modern off-shore shrimping industry.

The past and present merge at the junction of Centre and Front Streets. The 1899 Train Depot, replacing an earlier structure destroyed by the 1898 hurricane, now serves as the headquarters of the Tourist Development Council. While a vintage railroad car no longer stands guard, a CSX engine still forges ahead to the commercial docks on the pathway of the original tracks. As David Levy Yulee envisioned, the rails and the harbor are in perpetual harmony.

Looking as if it were a city unto itself, the industrial complex of Smurfit-Stone Container Corporation was constructed between Old Town and Fernandina Beach. Since 1936 their liner board and other products have served international and domestic clients. They have proven to be good stewards of the natural resources they harvest to create their pulp products.

Since 1939, Rayonier Corporation and its Performance Fibers Mill has been a vital partner in the survival of the local economy. It is seen here from Little Piney Island, looking across the Amelia River. Mountains of Southern pine chips are converted to chemical cellulose that appears in everything from plastics to ice cream. Sterilized vapor rises from the tall stacks.

By traveling down 14th Street to the North end of the island, you will discover Old Town, the last town platted by Spain in the Western Hemisphere in 1811. Before the eight flags, this site was home to the Timucuans, our original settlers. The Italianate Posada San Carlos, built by the Bell brothers who were harbor pilots when they weren't constructing homes, has gazed upon the harbor since 1877. In more recent times this home was featured in the film, "Pippi Longstocking." Production companies continue to choose Amelia Island for their movies.

The abandoned Nassau Fertilizer and Oil Company plant, as seen from Old Town, represents a once thriving industry. Fishermen set out in the early morning to catch menhaden (Brevoortia tyrannus), commonly referred to as "pogies", a major commercial fish. The catch was brought back and processed for fish oil, meal and solubles, which ended up in products that ranged from linoleum and paint, to oleo and salad dressing.

The past is seldom far from the present on Amelia Island. Tabby walls enclose some of the earlier plots in Bosque Bello Cemetery. Translated from the Spanish as "Beautiful Woods," it was said to have been established in 1798. Located on 14th Street in close proximity to Old Town, it is but one of many cemeteries on the island that genealogists have spent countless hours exploring and documenting.

SACRED
To the Memory of
MATILDA SETON
Wife of
CHARLES SETON ESQ
A native of Philadelphia
Who departed this life
The 17th September 1856.
Aged 64 Years
Blessed are the dead who die

Drive back through time. On the South end of the island, a brief stretch of the Buccaneer Trail becomes a cool oasis on the hottest of days.

Live Oaks intertwine their branches over the roadway. Spanish moss completes this evocation of the Old South.

Beach & Club Properties

Chapter VI

Our Brown Pelican continues his search to discover the treasures of Amelia Island.

The Ritz-Carlton, Amelia Island, where "ladies and gentlemen serve ladies and gentlemen." Since 1991 this AAA Five-Diamond and Mobil Four-Star resort has been the destination of choice for discerning guests. It offers an oceanside gourmet restaurant named "Salt", a new spa sports lounge called "Eight" and "Our Space", a unique teen zone. From families to conventions, guests can enjoy their time by the ocean surrounded by exquisite works of art and antiques, or venture out to explore the wonders of the island.

The 18th tee of The Golf Club of Amelia Island frames a view of the Carlton Dunes Condominiums and the Ritz-Carlton. Designed by Mark McCumber and Gene Littler, this is one of six courses on the island, with three more in close proximity.

The 12th green at the Amelia River Golf Club, designed by Tom Jackson, is the most recent addition to a stunning selection of island golfing opportunities.

The Fernandina Beach Golf Club, a public course, showcases the recently remodeled clubhouse, which presides over 27 golf holes designed by Ed Matteson and Tommy Birdsong. (The 9th green of the West Course is visible to the right.)

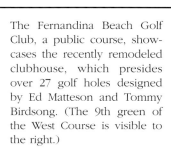

On the South end of the island, just off A1A, Burney Park offers handicapped accessible rest rooms, showers and a beach ramp. Another similar facility, Peter's Point, is off Fletcher Avenue. Burney Park is named after one of the founders of the Afro-American Insurance Company and marks the southern boundary of American Beach. Founded in 1935 by A. L. Lewis, this community was created as a resort by African-Americans, for African-Americans. It is listed on the Black History Trail.

The South end of the island was the site of one of the early African-American settlements. An active congregation meets regularly at the Franklintown United Methodist Church on Lewis Street in American Beach.

From 1972, inspired by the vision of Charles Fraser, a developer on Hilton Head Island, the Amelia Island Plantation has grown to include world class resort amenities. From golf and tennis to fine dining, a Nature Center, shopping and miles of pristine beaches, guests and residents can pursue their own particular pleasure in a setting of spectacular natural beauty. If your preference is for a luxurious hotel rather than one of the rental options, the elegant Amelia Island Inn, seen here on its oceanfront site, is for you.

While some Plantation residents have built private homes on a wide variety of sites, others have chosen condominiums like the ones pictured here. To the right is Sea Dunes, followed by Piper Dunes and finally, Windsong. The names are poetry, the views sublime.

The Ocean Club is an example of one of the many benefits of Plantation living. The crash of the surf is just steps away from the fresh water pool and patio.

Savor the view to the ocean from the 6th green of the Plantation's Ocean Links, designed by Pete Dye and Bobby Weed. By maintaining and enhancing the natural environment, golfers and naturalists have much to enjoy, from the bright blossoms of the Blanket Flower (Gaillardia pulchella) to the tall grassy fronds of Hairawn Muhly (Muhlenbergia capillaris).

For more than 20 years, the Bausch & Lomb Championships have brought top women pros to the courts at Amelia Island Plantation. From the Qualifying Rounds to the Championship and Local Pro Invitational Finals, there are nine full days of exciting singles and doubles tennis action. Seen above is Venus Williams; below, Amelie Mauresmo.

Three golfers (Homo erectus golfus) are concentrating on sinking the perfect putt. They are seen across the 9th Green of the Plantation's Oak Marsh course designed by Pete Dye.

Southern Magnolia (Magnolia grandiflora) trunks host Asiatic Jasmine (Trachelospermum asiaticum) vines and offer shade to Holly Ferns (Cyrtomium falcatum) flourishing in the left mid-range of this photograph. While it might be a naturalist's dream, it is also a golfer's nightmare when searching for an errant ball.

The Marsh & Wildlife

Chapter VII

Our Brown Pelican stands firm in his resolution that no tour of Amelia Island is complete without a closer look at the marshes and wildlife.

Peering out from the maritime forest with its border sentinel of a Live Oak, the wide vista of a salt marsh invites investigation. In the foreground are Saw Palmettoes (Serenoa repens), and, to the extreme left, a large bush of Yaupon Holly (Ilex vomitoria). Those of you who have read the first chapter know the secret of Yaupon and what this plant meant to the Timucuans.

A similar scene, with a most appropriately named plant on the left side: Spanish Dagger (Yucca aloifolia). The Spanish controlled the destiny of Amelia Island for 236 years. In an attempt to simplify our complex history, the observation has been made that "...the French visited, the Spanish developed, the English named and the Americans tamed." We are fortunate since we have only to savor and preserve!

Beat the Bees! Seemingly suspended in mid-air, a Ruby-Throated Hummingbird (Archilochus colubris), prepares to drink deeply from a waiting blossom's abundance of nectar. This is the only Eastern species.

Nature and man in harmony: an Oak Point pond offers resident birders a unique opportunity. The dark fellow perched on the point is a Double-Crested Cormorant (Phalacrocorax auritus), while the smaller pair of salt-and-pepper visitors in the center are immature White Ibis (Eudocimus albus). The four elegant observers are Great Egrets (Ardea alba).

Male (left) and female (right) nestlings needing a "nosh." This family of Pileated Woodpeckers (Dryocopus pileatus) has made their home in a tree trunk. The mature male (top) knows that his young family is ready for another meal. The mature female (bottom) obliges. Was it ever thus?

In the heart of the maritime forest a furred, masked bandit spies a fellow creature grasping a small, rectangular box in his "paws." Ever so slowly, the box is lifted to the upper portion of a maskless, furless face. The Common Raccoon (Procyon lotor) is mesmerized by this strange behavior. Experience has taught him to expect the unexpected from humans. CLICK…and down the trunk and into the underbrush he disappears, before Roger has a second chance.

Nature and the built environment coexist in harmony. Condominiums can be seen on the horizon, while the salt marsh continues to support an eco-system that has flourished for millennia. In the larger photograph, a Great Egret is poised below, while a Great Blue Heron (Ardea herodias) is camouflaged in the mid-distance.

A Great Horned Owl (Bubo virginianus) stands guard over the next generation. The twisted branches of an oak provide shelter and protection from predators. The owlets are curious, but the watchful parent will stand by until they are ready to leave the safe haven of their nest.

A Great Blue Heron poses, dockside. For a brief moment he appears earthbound; yet within his spirit lies the potential to ride the wind. Whether as nature made him, or sculpted in bronze or caught in the camera's eye, he is a metaphor that represents all that is both permanent and fleeting in this life.

At times the island's air literally vibrates with a symphony of sounds from the Green Treefrog (Hyla cinerea). Once you have heard it, the musical memory will be yours to keep forever.